THE PONY
HOBBY BOOK

British Library Cataloguing-in-Publication Data.
A catalogue record for this book is available from
the British Library.

ISBN 0.85131.639.5

© J.A.Allen & Co. Ltd.

No part of this book may be reproduced, stored in
a retrieval system, or transmitted, in any form or by
any means, electronic, mechanical, photocopying,
recording or otherwise, without the prior
permission of the publisher. All rights reserved.

Published in Great Britain in 1995 by
J.A.Allen & Company Limited,
1 Lower Grosvenor Place,
Buckingham Palace Road,
London, SW1W 0EL.

Typeset by Setrite Typesetters Ltd., Hong Kong
Printed by Dah Hua Printing Press Co. Ltd., Hong Kong

Designed by Nancy Lawrence

THE PONY HOBBY BOOK

KAREN BUSH   CLAIRE COLVIN

J.A.ALLEN
LONDON

INTRODUCTION

Yet another birthday has gone by. Everyone has ignored your ever-so-subtle hints, and you still haven't woken up to find a pony waiting for you at the bottom of the garden. Well it's no good crying over it. Maybe you can't afford a pony (or to keep it, which is even more expensive) or perhaps you live in an area where there just aren't suitable facilities. It doesn't mean that you'll necessarily be ponyless forever, though you might have to wait ages before you realise your dream – perhaps even until you've left school and have a job. If you're determined and patient enough, you will get one in the end, really you will. In the meantime you just have to make the best of it and, believe it or not, there are loads of horsy things to do, see and join which you definitely don't need a pony for.

Of course, you might be one of the lucky ones and have a pony already, in which case there's really no excuse for moping around the house saying you're bored and haven't anything to do. Assuming, however, that you've been super efficient and have groomed, ridden, mucked out, checked the fencing, tidied the muckheap, cleaned your tack, spring-cleaned the stable and done all the hundred and one other things that need doing and still have a spare five minutes on your hands, you might also like to try out some of the ideas in this book.

BEFORE YOU START...

VERY IMPORTANT!

• Never cut, paint, or glue directly onto table surfaces; put down newspaper first and use a wooden board beneath your project if cutting with a craft knife.
• Always use craft knives, scissors and other sharp cutting tools **away** from you and don't get your fingers in the way. With tricky items, ask an adult to help you.
• If pins and needles are needed, always put them safely away in a tin or pincushion when not using them. Don't leave them lying around; if the dog doesn't swallow them first, you can guarantee someone will end up standing on one!
• If you are prone to stabbing yourself with a needle when working on something which needs some stitching, use a thimble or ask an adult to help you.

PONY PIN-UPS

Instead of buying a calendar, you could make your own for a change using your favourite pictures cut from magazines, or, to add a personal touch, photos of a favourite pony.

YOU WILL NEED:
12 pieces of paper, all the same size
12 pictures
Stapler
Glue
Hole puncher
Short piece of wool, cord or ribbon
Small calendar booklet for next year (you can buy these cheaply from stationers).

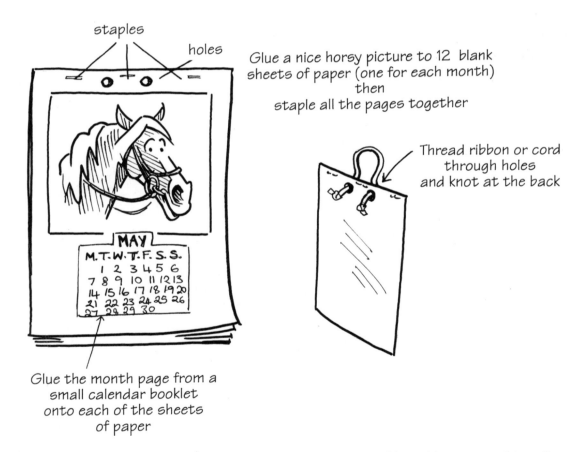

staples

holes

Glue a nice horsy picture to 12 blank sheets of paper (one for each month) then staple all the pages together

Thread ribbon or cord through holes and knot at the back

MAY
M. T. W. T. F. S. S.

Glue the month page from a small calendar booklet onto each of the sheets of paper

Glue a picture or photo on each piece of paper together with a page from the calendar booklet. Staple the sheets together at the top. Make two holes with the hole punch and thread the cord, ribbon or wool through them, knotting it at the back, and it's ready to hang up.

PONY BEANBAGS

A family of pony beanbags can be a lot of fun and a real talking point. Arrange them on a shelf, on your bed, or teach yourself to juggle with them; they'll keep you company wherever you go, sitting on your knee, or popped into a pocket, and make brilliant presents for friends.

You won't be able to avoid having to do a bit of sewing (mums with sewing machines will come in handy), but even stitched by hand beanbags don't take long to make and are well worth the effort.

YOU WILL NEED:

Material   Don't be tempted to cut up the bedroom curtains, but ask an adult if there are any old scraps lying around which you can use. Alternatively you can buy scraps of leftover oddments cheaply from fabric shops.

Felt scraps

Glue suitable for use on fabric.

Fun fur

Needle, thread and a few pins

Sheet of newspaper

Felt tip pen, or tailors' chalk if you use a dark coloured material.

Rice or pearl barley

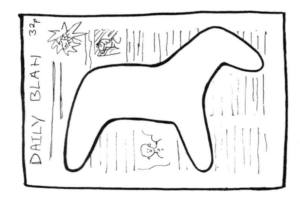

1. Draw out a simple pony shape like this on a piece of newspaper, then cut it out. Do not make the legs or neck too long or thin.

1. Draw out a pony shape on a piece of newspaper to make a pattern, but don't be tempted to make the neck too long (the head will flop about too much if you do), or the legs very thin otherwise you'll have trouble turning them inside out and stuffing them later on. When you've drawn the pony, cut it out following the lines carefully and then pin it to the wrong (unprinted) side of a piece of fabric.

Draw round the outline with a felt tip pen (or piece of chalk) trying not to stretch the fabric as you do so, or you'll end up with an odd shape. Remove the pins and the pattern and cut out the shape, leaving a 6.4 mm (1/4 in) margin of extra material round the outside of your lines.

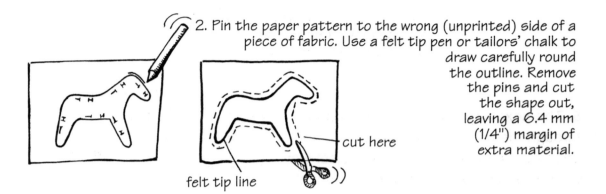

2. Pin the paper pattern to the wrong (unprinted) side of a piece of fabric. Use a felt tip pen or tailors' chalk to draw carefully round the outline. Remove the pins and cut the shape out, leaving a 6.4 mm (1/4") margin of extra material.

felt tip line

cut here

2. Make a second fabric shape in the same way, but reverse the paper pattern before drawing round it so that you end up with a left- and a right-hand side instead of two left- or two right-hand sides.

3. Turn the pattern over so it faces in the opposite direction and make a second fabric shape as before.

3. Pin the two pieces of material together with the right (printed) sides facing each other and carefully sew along the edges using the lines you made with the pen or chalk as a guide. Use backstitch (shown in the picture), making your stitches as small and neat as possible so your filling can't escape through any gaps. Leave a gap of about 5 cm (2 in) in length along the back so you can turn it inside out and fill it.

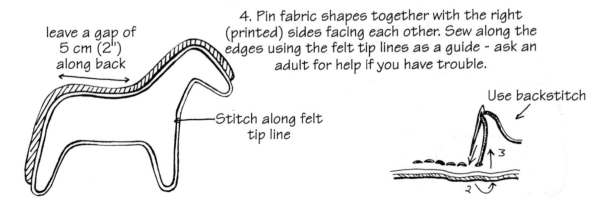

leave a gap of 5 cm (2") along back

4. Pin fabric shapes together with the right (printed) sides facing each other. Sew along the edges using the felt tip lines as a guide - ask an adult for help if you have trouble.

Stitch along felt tip line

Use backstitch

4. Remove all the pins and turn the beanbag inside out (or right way round!); be patient because it takes a little while and you don't want to tear the stitches or material. Use a knitting needle or pencil to help push out the really fiddly bits where fingers can't reach, such as the legs.

5. Turn the shape inside out, using a knitting needle or pencil to push out the legs, neck and head.

Making a paper funnel:

Sellotape

Roll up a piece of paper or thin card to make a conical funnel shape. Use a piece of Sellotape to stop it unravelling

5. The next step is to fill your beanbag through the hole you have left, using the dried rice or pearl barley. The easiest way to do this is to use a small plastic funnel, doing a little at a time so you can shake it down into the legs and head. If you don't have a funnel, roll up a piece of paper to form a cone shape and use a piece of sellotape to stop it from unravelling itself. No matter how careful you are, you'll find that some of the rice or barley always seems to manage to escape, so do it over a sheet of newspaper to catch it. Don't overdo the filling because beanbags are meant to be a bit floppy and it will also make it difficult to sew the last seam up.

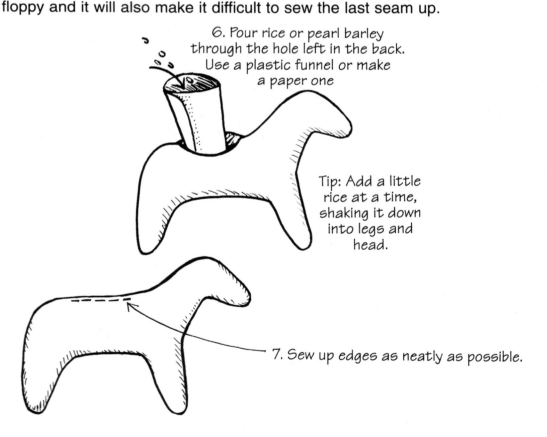

6. Pour rice or pearl barley through the hole left in the back. Use a plastic funnel or make a paper one

Tip: Add a little rice at a time, shaking it down into legs and head.

7. Sew up edges as neatly as possible.

6. Sew up the remaining hole as neatly as possible, turning the edges of the material inwards so no frayed edges show. The seam will be slightly raised, but this is easily disguised by cutting out a felt saddle shape and using a little fabric glue along the seam to hold it in place.

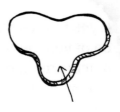

Cut out a felt saddle shape ...

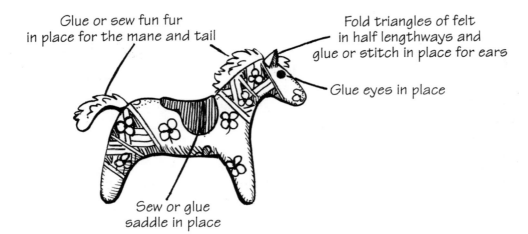

Glue or sew fun fur in place for the mane and tail

Fold triangles of felt in half lengthways and glue or stitch in place for ears

Glue eyes in place

Sew or glue saddle in place

Finally, add the finishing touches: a strip of fun fur for the mane and tail, held in place with a few stitches, and glue on two circles of felt for the eyes.

...two felt eyes ...

Ears can be made by folding two triangles of felt in half lengthways and gluing or stitching them into place.

... and two felt ears - plus 2 short strips of fun fur fabric

8. The finished product - make it any size you like! For really big bean bags you can sit on, ask an adult to sew along the edges with a sewing machine, and fill with polystyrene beads.

If you're a bit more ambitious, once you get the hang of it, try making an underside for the tummy and legs to create a more three-dimensional beanbag.

3-D BEANBAGS

This is a more ambitious project, and you may need to ask an adult to help you if you want to make a 3-D beanbag with four legs instead of two.

- - -Fold line- - -

You will need a gusset this shape for the tummy and inside of the legs. Use the paper pattern for the sides to help get the right shape and size.

This is what it should look like when finished.

When you have cut out the two sides, cut the pattern in half like this.

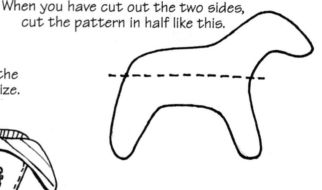

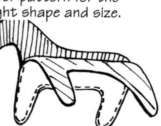

Sew in the gusset first

Add a small triangular shape here before cutting out.

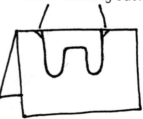

Place the new shape at the top edge of a folded piece of newspaper. Trace around the shape and cut out. When you unfold the paper you should have a pattern for the gusset.

Have a go at making a bigger beanbag you can sit on, filling it with polystyrene beads instead of rice or barley. Because of its size, you'll probably need some help from someone with a sewing machine!

TESTING TIMES

If you thought horsy exams were only for adults planning careers with equines, think again. There are numerous exams you can study for, and they're a lot more fun than school exams because they're all about a subject closer to your heart than geography or maths. If you want to work with horses when you leave school, they can provide a really good foundation and might even help to give you a leg up when it comes to getting a job or place at a training centre.

Even if you don't have plans for a horsy career, taking exams is a great way of assessing your progress, and you'll have some really concrete goals to aim for, not to mention some impressive certificates to stick up on your bedroom walls afterwards!

ABRS WEEKLY RIDER TESTS

If you ride at an Association of British Riding Schools (ABRS) approved school, ask your instructor if you can work towards the series of ABRS Weekly Rider Equitation and Stable Management Tests. These are designed especially for riding school customers who don't have their own horses or ponies. The tests start at a very basic level suitable for beginners, and they must be taken in order; when you have passed the first test you can apply to take the next one as soon as your instructor thinks you are ready for it.

Each test costs a little more than an extra lesson and can be taken at your own riding school on ponies you know and are used to riding or caring for. Most riding schools will gear lessons towards the tests, and offer short courses and lectures beforehand to ensure you are properly prepared. Booklets containing details of what you will be expected to do for each test are available for a small charge from: The General Secretary, Association of British Riding Schools, Old Brewery Yard, Penzance, Cornwall, TR18 2SL.

BRITISH HORSE SOCIETY (BHS) HORSE OWNERS CERTIFICATE

If your big ambition in life is to own a pony one day, this might be just the exam for you. There are three levels, each of which is aimed at making sure you have all the necessary knowledge to care for a horse or pony properly (not to mention making sure that you know how to go about buying the right one in the first place!).

Rather than a practical exam, it takes the form of a one and a half hour written paper which is set and marked by a member of the British Horse Society Register of Instructors, who will run a course beforehand. Because it is quite a long written test, the BHS suggests candidates should be a minimum age of 12 to take the exam, but, to an extent, this depends on how academic you are. Details of the exam and costs are available from the Examinations Office, British Horse Society, British Equestrian Centre, Stoneleigh, Kenilworth, Warwickshire CV8 2LR.

Some exams can be fun - ask
at your riding school about the
horsy tests you can take

RIDING CLUBS JUNIOR GRADE TESTS

Riding clubs which are affiliated to the British Horse Society run graded tests specifically for their members. Most riding clubs have a section for junior members, aged between eight and 17 years, who can take tests graded from I to III. If you do not own a pony, you will need to either hire or borrow one for the day. Exam days and lessons/lectures in preparation for taking the tests are arranged by each riding club, and you should ask the Secretary for details.

RIDING AND ROAD SAFETY EXAM

If you ride on the roads at all, you should really think seriously about taking the BHS Riding and Road Safety Exam, it will help you to be better equipped to deal with the kind of traffic conditions most riders have to put up with today. If you are a member of the Pony Club or a BHS affiliated riding club, ask the Secretary for details. Sometimes riding schools will arrange training sessions and tests for their clients or, alternatively, contact the British Horse Society at the address given.

BHS PROGRESSIVE RIDING TESTS

Like the ABRS tests, these are designed for riding-school customers, and cover both riding and stable management, They are administered by BHS approved schools, and you should ask your instructor for information.

PONY CLUB TESTS

The Pony Club runs a series of seven graded tests covering riding and stable management. You will first have to become a member of a local branch of the Pony Club, after which you will be actively encouraged to take the tests. Although you do not have to own a pony, you will need to either hire or borrow a pony for the test day. Details about the Pony Club and the tests are available from the Pony Club which is also based at The British Equestrian Centre.

TIP: If you adapt an existing board game to a horsy one, use sticky Post-it notes rather than gluing paper directly onto playing boards - they are easily removed later.

Try making your own horsy board games

Fed up with the same old board games? Fancy something which has a more horsy feel to it? There are several horsy board games that you can buy, but if your money won't stretch that far there is no reason why you can't invent your own or else adapt existing games you already have.

Try playing Scrabble for instance, but using only horsy words, or words which could be applied to something horsy. For example, you can use the word 'fall' providing you make it clear that it refers to a fall from a pony or horse, or 'log' as in a log fence on a cross-country course. It'll test your ingenuity and ability to be 100 per cent pony mad!

You can adapt Cluedo by changing the names of the characters to those of horsy personalities or friends, and the murder weapons to things you would find lying around in a stable yard – pitchfork, lead rope, and so on. The names of the rooms should be horsy too – tack room, stable, feed room, indoor school – or whatever you fancy, then simply play the game along the usual lines.

With Monopoly, change the names of the properties to those of riding schools and trekking centres (real or fictitious), and instead of buying houses and hotels, pretend they are stables and indoor schools. Make some new Chance cards to fit in with the theme, including things like 'Fall into water jump at Badminton, go back to leading-rein class' (the Jail square) and similar ideas.

Don't deface the board completely because you might want to go back to the original format, so use easily removable sticky labels such as Post-it notes if you want to change the property names.

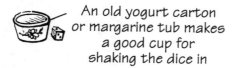 An old yogurt carton or margarine tub makes a good cup for shaking the dice in

 Use buttons or small model horses as playing pieces

If you have a good imagination you can make up your own board games too. All you will need is a large piece of stiff card to make a playing board and some paints to colour it with, plus one or two dice and a few counters – small plastic model horses are ideal. Work out your idea on some scrap paper first; something simple but effective perhaps, such as moving the playing pieces along numbered squares according to the number thrown on the dice. Add a few hazard and bonus squares and then invite a few friends round to try it out!

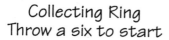 You can make your own horsy board games like this.

Collecting Ring
Throw a six to start

Use a dice - the number thrown will decide how many squares forwards each player moves along the board

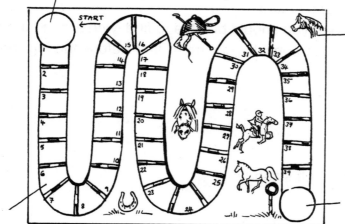

Draw and paint pony pics on the board

Finish - Trophy Tent!

Add penalty and bonus squares:
eg. fall off your pony - go back to Collecting Ring
   OR: Jump a clear round - go forward two squares

HORSE IN THE HOUSE

Buy a horse or pony in the colour of your choice for less than a fiver! OK, so it isn't a real one, but when you're desperate it's better than nothing. It would still look pretty good in a corner of your bedroom, but if you feel you're really a bit old for a hobby horse, there's nothing to stop you from making it for a younger brother, sister or relative.

The most expensive part is the broom handle you will need for mounting the head on; it's not a good idea to sabotage the brand new kitchen mop for the bits you want, so ask if there is an old one buried under the stairs which isn't used any more. If not, trot down to your nearest hardware store and buy a handle (they can be bought minus the bristly broom head), it shouldn't cost more than a pound or two, so it won't break the bank completely. If you find that the handle is a bit long, ask someone to cut it to the length you want and sandpaper the end smooth.

Everything else you need you should be able to find lying around the house, although it might be wise to consult your mum first before turning the place upside down looking.

YOU WILL NEED:
1 large sock, preferably adult sized.
Wool
Two buttons
Darning needle
Felt or material scraps
Stuffing   Tights, stockings or foam rubber cut up into small pieces, or kapok.
Elastic   Approximately 30 cm (12 in) long, 6.4 cm (1/4 in) wide (8 cord).
Cotton thread
Sewing needle

1. The first thing to do is make sure that the sock you have chosen is clean (or the smell might just drive everyone else outside) and without holes through which the stuffing could leak out. Having done this, thread a length of the cotton thread onto the sewing needle, push one hand into the sock and with the other sew the buttons on to the foot of the sock, just below the heel, to make the eyes. Use a matching colour thread, unless you prefer a more spirited expression, in which case try white cotton instead. Take care not to place the buttons too close together or your hobby horse will look as though it has a squint!

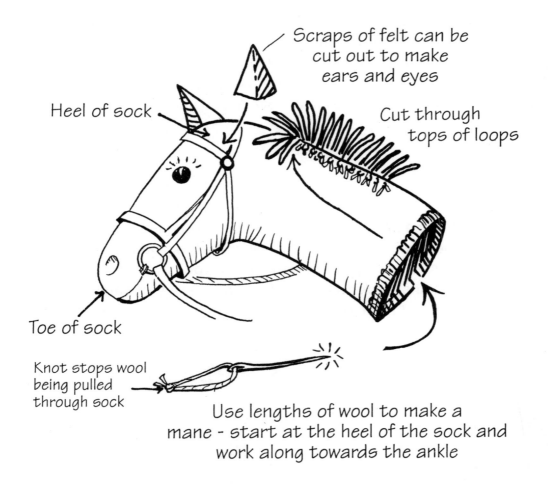

Scraps of felt can be cut out to make ears and eyes

Heel of sock

Cut through tops of loops

Toe of sock

Knot stops wool being pulled through sock

Use lengths of wool to make a mane - start at the heel of the sock and work along towards the ankle

2. Now cut out two triangular pieces of felt or material, fold them in half lengthways and stitch them into place on either side of the heel of the sock to make the ears.

3. The next step will need a bit of patience. Thread the darning needle with a length of wool and tie a knot in the end so that it can't be pulled right through the sock material. Put one hand in the sock, scrunching the open end up to make things easier and push the needle through from the inside to the outside, drawing the wool through after it. Having pulled the wool through, cut it off to roughly the length you want, and then repeat the process – if you're smart, you'll use a doubled length each time with the two ends of the wool knotted together. This will give you two strands of mane at a time. Work your way like this from the heel down to the ankle of the sock so that all the emerging strands form a mane. How thick and long it is depends on how much patience (and wool) you have. Lazy types who hate sewing could always skip this part and pretend that it's been hogged!

4. The interesting part where everything takes shape happens next. Stuff the sock with the nylon tights, foam or kapok and then insert the broom handle into the ankle, trying not to lose all the filling in the process. Tie the elastic tightly over the end of the sock (ask someone to put a finger on the knot so it doesn't slip), trim the ends off and then tuck it all upwards into the base of the stuffed 'neck' so it doesn't show. Finally, trim the mane neatly to its final length, and make a bridle using scraps of felt and material and gluing (or stitching) them in place.

GLOVE PUPPET

As a variation on the hobby-horse theme, you can make horsy glove puppets by following the same procedure as above, but omitting the stuffing and broom handle, and remembering that if you have small hands, you will need to sew on the ears and eyes slightly further forward. When you have finished, simply put your hand inside the sock with your knuckles facing upwards and thumb beneath; then dimple the toe of the sock inwards between fingers and thumb to make a mouth.

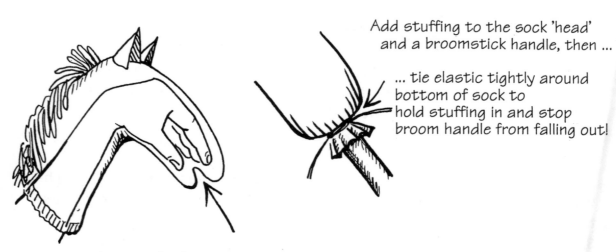

Add stuffing to the sock 'head' and a broomstick handle, then ...

... tie elastic tightly around bottom of sock to hold stuffing in and stop broom handle from falling out!

Instead of a hobby horse, you could try making a glove puppet instead - leave out the filling and broom handle.

THE SILLY NAME GAME

This really is a silly game, good for parties, evenings at Pony Club camp, or if you just have a few friends round and can't think of anything better to do with your time. It's very simple; you invent your own library of imaginary bestselling horsy books. You can each think of a title and author, or take it in turns to propose a title whilst the others try to come up with a really appropriate author. Set a time limit for suggestions, and the silliest (or cleverest) is the winner. Here are a few to get you started.

Feeding Ponies by A. Net and Molly Chaff.
The Pony Who Wouldn't be Caught by Lucinda Field.
Equine Influenza by Willie Catchit.
Livery Fees by Bill Overdue.
Learn to Ride by G. Up.
Commentating on Horses by Ann Ouncer.
Which? Jodhpurs by Lucy Lastic.

TURN YOUR BEDROOM INTO A STABLE

Are you fed up with all those sarcastic comments about the state of your bedroom? Have you had enough of being sent upstairs to go and tidy it when you would far rather be down at the stables mucking out Snowy's luxury apartment instead? Obviously it's time you did something about it. Turn your bedroom into a stable – it will be more fun keeping it tidy and will silence all those complaints for ever.

MUCK OUT

First things first. Clear up all that stuff lying around on the floor; retrieve your jodhs from under the bed and throw away that mouldy, half-eaten Mars bar for starters. Having made a bit of space on the floor, wheel out the Hoover and give the carpet a good once over; if it all sounds suspiciously like housework so far, just remember that, as any good horseperson will tell you, a well-kept stable is a tidy one, not an obstacle course.

A dusty environment is also an unhealthy one, so nip round with a duster, and remove that huge spider's web lurking in the corner – dusty webs don't catch flies, only more dust.

With a little imagination you can turn your
bedroom into a horsy heaven!

STABLE DOOR

Every stable needs a decent door. This part might prove a bit tricky because your parents probably consider the one you have already to be perfectly adequate.

Empty your piggy bank, do a bit of car washing or weeding to earn the extra cash needed and then, using your most persuasive techniques, ask if you can buy a stable-style split door from your local DIY superstore. They are not as expensive as you would imagine, and don't forget to point out to your parents how tasteful they can look. If you succeed in wearing down the inevitable resistance to the idea, try not to succumb to the temptation to imitate your favourite pony by kicking at the bottom half of the door every morning at breakfast time, or you just might find Dad regretting fitting it for you in the first place.

If a stable door is out of the question, don't panic, improvise instead. You can buy sheets of sticky-backed plastic or vinyl with a wood panelling look which, with a little bit of smart scissor work, you can cut to size to make an imitation stable door on the inside – which is where it really matters.

For a finishing touch, you could buy a giant poster of a horse's head to stick on the top half of your door so it looks as though he is peering in.

SKEPPING OUT

A well-kept stable needs to be regularly skepped out if it isn't to become a health hazard. Plastic mesh laundry baskets bought from hardware stores are just the thing to use as skeps. Use yours to chuck your dirty washing in.

Laundry basket/skep

NAMEPLATE

If you really want to go to town, make a nameplate for the outside of your stable door, just like they have in really smart yards. You'll find instructions for doing this elsewhere in this book.

BITS 'N' PIECES

In saddlers and junk shops keep an eye out for second-hand horsy bits and pieces such as bits, parts of bridles, headcollars and horse brasses. They don't need to be in perfect condition since they won't be doing anything more strenuous than looking decorative and adding to the horsy feel of your room, so can be fairly cheap to buy.

Washed and gleaming after a bit of spit and polish, they will really look the part, particularly if you hang them on the walls from horseshoe nails. Ask your local farrier for a couple, but let your dad nail them in for you to ensure you don't accidentally hit an electric cable.

FEED

Lots of pony owners keep their feeds in plastic dustbins to help keep it dry and mouseproof. There's no reason why you shouldn't do the same, on a smaller scale. Scrounge some feed samples from friends and buy a set of the small plastic dustbins sold in stationers as desk tidies to keep them in, then label the lids according to the contents, e.g. nuts, oats, barley. It is also a very good way of learning how to identify feeds correctly.

Make your own set of mini feed bins

GRAZING

Admittedly grazing is not found in stables, but a bit of 'grass' will help to give your room a more horsy feel (unless you already have a straw- or shavings-coloured carpet). See if you can beg a piece of artificial grass from a greengrocer to spread on the floor instead of a rug.

GROOMING KIT

There is no point in looking scruffy. Buy a plastic grooming-kit box from a saddlers or hardware shop for your dressing table to hold all your personal 'grooming kit': comb, hairbrush, nail clippers, shampoo, hair grips etc.

Personal grooming kit

Hoof oil pencil tidy

PENCIL TIDY

Use an old hoof oil tin or tub as a pen or pencil tidy. Make sure you wash it out thoroughly first, but be careful to leave the labelling intact. You could also use an old saddle soap tin in which to keep odds and ends tidy. If you don't use saddle soap or hoof oil because you don't own a pony, ask a pony owning friend, or at your local riding school, for the containers when they're empty.

SWEET DREAMS

A comfortable bed is a must in any stable, but that doesn't mean you have to cover your mattress with a bale of straw. Apart from the fact that your parents will probably take a pretty dim view of it, it's very scratchy. Buy (or ask for one as a present) a horsy duvet cover. Alternatively buy a second-hand horse rug, give it a clean and use it as a bedspread. Day rugs look especially good, particularly if you add your initials to the corner; you can make your own, or buy felt letters from saddlers for a few pence.

ALL HUNG UP

You wouldn't leave Snowy's rugs lying around on the floor, so don't just drop your jackets there either! Mount a bridle hook on the wall to use as a clothes peg.

KEEPING TIDY

Water bucket waste paper bin

To succeed in keeping your new horsy room tidy, you really ought to have somewhere (apart from the floor) to put your rubbish. Instead of a wastepaper basket, keep to the general theme by using a plastic water bucket – if you're feeling really enterprising and your parents don't object, you could even mount it in a metal water bucket holder fixed to the wall.

JUMP POLES

A few jump poles might look good too, although, obviously, the real thing might be a bit cumbersome. Collect the cardboard tubes from the centre of loo rolls or kitchen towels and give them a coat of paint. Then sellotape the ends together, alternating the colours and, presto, your own jump poles. Lay them out on the floor as trotting poles, or rest the ends on cardboard boxes to make a show jump, but stack them tidily in a corner when they're not in use.

Paint the cardboard centres of loo rolls or kitchen towels - then sellotape ends together to make a set of jump or trotting poles

HORSE IN THE HOUSE

No stable is complete without a horse, although you might conceivably have problems trying to smuggle a real one up the stairs without anyone noticing. There are ways round this: start a collection of model horses, dig out the old rocking horse from the attic, or make a hobby horse to keep you company.

PUZZLE IT OUT

If you're a jigsaw addict, chances are you're bored with doing the ones you already have over and over again. On the other hand, maybe the idea of sitting still for more than five minutes to put a jigsaw together makes you squirm, especially if it is a less than thrilling picture of a country cottage without even a single pony browsing in the herbaceous border to liven it all up. If the subject matter were more inspiring, however, you might possibly be just a little more interested.

If you have a favourite horsy poster or magazine poster but no more room to stick anything else on your bedroom walls, why not convert it into a jigsaw? If you really cannot stand the thought of reassembling it yourself afterwards, it can make a good present for a horsy friend.

Glue a picture on to a piece of card; once it is dry, use scissors or a craft knife to cut out jigsaw puzzle shapes.

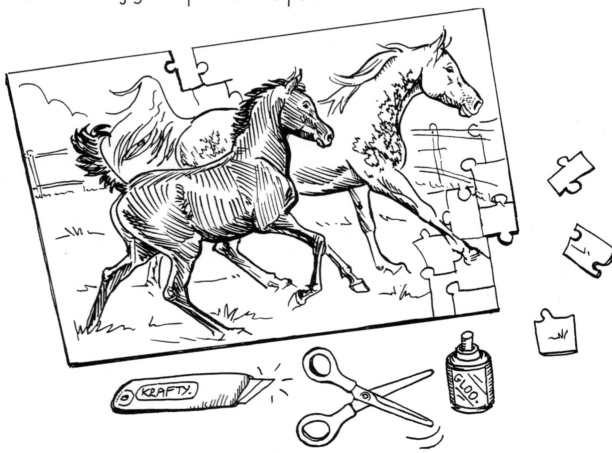

YOU WILL NEED:
A nice picture
Paper glue
Cardboard   You can buy this from good art shops. Don't go for very thick card as you'll find it hard to cut easily.

1. Glue the picture onto the card, making sure that covers all the paper, and carefully smooth out any wrinkles or air bubbles, working from the centre of the picture towards the outside edges. Remember that paper covered in glue does tend to get soggy and will tear easily if you are too impatient with it. With very big pictures you may also find it easiest to cut them up into manageable sections first before gluing them into place, but make sure you match the edges together properly.

2. Leave it all to dry completely before making the jigsaw pieces, using a pair of sharp scissors or a craft knife to cut them out. Draw out the shapes in advance if you like (use a very fine-pointed pencil) or just get stuck into it, making it up as you go along. Make it as easy or as difficult as you like by cutting bigger or smaller pieces. You can make wiggly shapes, or, better still, just do straight lines because this can make it more challenging to put together again, particularly when doing the edges.

KEEPING POSTED

You are bound to get at least one horsy postcard this year – from a friend or relative on holiday perhaps – but instead of throwing them away once you've read the message and admired the picture, why not start a collection?

If you want to start collecting immediately, you don't of course have to wait until you (or someone else) goes on holiday, you can buy horsy postcards from lots of high street shops and newsagents as well as from breed societies and trade stands at horse shows. If you visit any museums or art galleries, don't forget to look in the gift shop before you leave, as you'll often find lovely postcards for sale with pictures of famous horse paintings and sculptures on them.

There are all sorts of pictures, ranging from head-and-shoulder portraits, to breeds, horses and ponies in harness, performing horses, and humorous ones, all of which you could divide into appropriate categories. In fact you'll probably find that once your collection begins to grow, unless you have unlimited space, it is best to specialise in a particular theme. Mount them in a scrapbook so that they don't get damaged, but use photo corners to enable you to remove them easily or change the order of them if you want, and make an index for easy reference. If you can get a friend interested in the idea as well, you can also arrange a few swops.

If you get really involved with postcard collecting as a hobby, you may decide to acquire some old postcards as well as modern ones; some have been around for nearly a hundred years. These will cost a little more to buy, pounds instead of pence, but as horses and ponies were really popular subjects in the early 1900s you'll have plenty of choice. Look out for them at jumble sales, in junk shops and antique shops, at car-boot sales and antique fairs. You'll find events like this advertised in your local newspaper.

Do try to pick up cards which are in fairly good condition if you buy old ones because you will find it easier to swop or sell them, and they will look nicer in your collection. If you have a browse through a copy of the *Stanley Gibbons Postcard Catalogue* (you should be able to find one in the reference section of your county library) it will give you a better idea of the sort of cards you can find and roughly how much they will cost.

SOUVENIR SHOES

A shoe from a favourite pony is a lovely memento, and can make a nice decoration for your bedroom. Ask the farrier if you can keep one next time he calls. If you don't own a pony but are especially fond of one at your riding school, ask your instructor if he/she will ask for a shoe for you. Front shoes are usually a nicer shape than back ones.

Thread ribbon through nail holes so you can hang the shoe up.

Paint or spray the shoe of a favourite pony

SNOWY

Use a fine artist's paintbrush to paint in the pony's name

Clean the shoe with a stiff, wire-bristled brush, and use a nail to clear the nail holes. Spread out a sheet of newspaper, place the shoe on top and use a gold or silver metallic lacquer aerosol to spray it. It is best to do this out of doors on a dry, still day because it can spread quite a distance, and your mum might not take kindly to half the furniture and most of the carpet changing colour! When it's dry, turn it over and spray the reverse side as well.

Using a fine artist's paint brush and a little gloss paint (see if there's any left over from decorating) carefully paint the pony's name along the toe – you might like to add the date as well. Thread a piece of ribbon through the topmost nail holes on each side, knotting it at the back of the shoe, then you'll be able to hang it up somewhere in your room.

SAVE A PONY

Instead of saving up for a pony, you could always try saving a pony instead. Your parents might take a pretty dim view of you actually rushing off and bringing home a rescue pony (especially if you were planning to graze him on the lawn and stable him in the garage) but there are lots of ways in which you can help horsy charities.

The charities work tirelessly to help horses, ponies and donkeys who are neglected or ill-treated, both in this country and abroad. Funds are always needed; without donations made by you and other caring people, they simply wouldn't be able to carry on. Raising money can be fun too, particularly if you get together with a few friends. Remember, no matter how big or small your contribution, every penny counts.

Do get your parents' permission before organising a fundraising event, and remember that it is not a good idea to collect money in a public place or door-to-door. Collecting in this way may not be very safe, and you would need to apply for permission from the local authority anyway. There are plenty of other things you can do though. You will probably be able to think up lots of ways in which to raise money, but here are a few ideas to get you started.

SPONSORED ACTIVITIES

You can be sponsored for doing almost anything, including:
• tack cleaning
• riding
• silences (popular with parents!)
• walks
• rug cleaning
• swimming
• bike rides.

Get yourself organised; make up a form (type it for neatness if possible) with the name of the charity you are trying to raise money for at the top, your name and address, what you are planning to do, and when. Draw columns under this in which your sponsors can put their names, addresses and how much they are going to sponsor you for. Some charities supply sponsorship forms, so it might be worth writing to enquire about this beforehand.

Ask everyone you know to sponsor you, explaining why the charity you are supporting needs help. After the event, get an adult to sign a piece of paper stating that you have succeeded in doing whatever you set out to do, and then contact your sponsors to collect what they owe you.

There are plenty of ways you can help support horsy charities. Try to involve your friends too - it is all in a good cause!

GIVE A PENNY FOR THE PONY

ADOPT A PONY

Most horse charities run 'adoption' schemes. In return for a small yearly dona-tion which is put towards feeding and caring for one of their horses, ponies or donkeys you are sent progress reports on him or her and a photo. You can also go to visit 'your' pony at the charity home. The minimum fees are usually quite small and certainly won't break the bank, but you can pay more if you want. Giving an 'adoption' pony to a horsy friend can make a great (and different) pre-sent too.

CARDS 'N' GIFTS

If you buy Christmas cards from a horse charity, you will know that your money is going to a good cause. As well as greetings cards, lots of charities also have gift catalogues with great presents to suit all pockets.

SAVE UP

Keep a special tin or box in which you can put some of your pocket money each week. If you give up eating sweets for a certain number of weeks as a spon-sored activity, the money you save could go into your collection box. Leave it in a prominent place in the house and encourage everyone else in your family to pop their small change in it too; before long you will have saved up quite a size-able amount.

If you go abroad on holiday, you may have some foreign currency left over which you can't spend and which is too small an amount to change at the bank, but some charities have an arrangement with their bank to exchange foreign coins. Make sure they are securely parcelled up before sending them off.

SECONDHAND SAVERS

Charity stalls can make quite a lot of money by selling your unwanted bits and pieces: books, games, bric-a-brac, outgrown clothes (even house and garden plants are in demand, but you'd better ask before digging up your dad's prize rosebushes!). Unwanted rugs, saddlery and other equipment may often be welcome, but it must be safe and in good condition.

JOIN UP!

Another way of helping is to become a charity member; many charities run special clubs for younger supporters. You will receive regular newsletters, can find out what other members have been doing, and enter competitions, all for a small subscription each year.

LEND A HAND

You can raise funds by making yourself useful too. Try offering to do some dog walking, baby sitting, car washing, lawn mowing or weeding.

SENDING YOUR DONATIONS

Don't send cash through the post; it is much safer to send it as a postal order or cheque.

THE CHARITIES

You can find out more about the work of horse charities and how you can help by writing to them; as well as those mentioned here you may find others advertised in newspapers and magazines. Do remember to enclose a stamped, self-addressed envelope if you require a reply, postage costs can soon mount up and the money could otherwise have been put to good use helping a needy horse, pony or donkey.

Ada Cole Memorial Stables, Broadlands, Broadley Common, Nr Nazeing, Waltham Abbey, Essex, EN9 2DH. Tel: (0199 289) 2133. Visiting times: every afternoon (except Christmas Day) 2 pm–5 pm. There is a sponsorship scheme, a junior club (The T.A.C. Club) and Christmas cards are available by mail order and at the stable gift shop. Horses, ponies and donkeys are loaned to approved homes.

Brooke Hospital for Animals, Broadmead House, 21 Panton Street, London, SW1Y 4DR. Tel: 0171-930 0210. The Brooke Hospital was founded to improve the lot of horses and donkeys in Egypt, Jordan, Pakistan and India. The charity has a Junior Club, and accepts petrol vouchers, tack and second-hand goods. Supporting material such as sponsor forms, ideas sheets, leaflets, badges, and collecting boxes are available if you are organising an event. Gifts and greetings cards by mail order.

Devon Horse & Pony Sanctuary, Manaton, Newton Abbot, Devon, TQ13 9UY. Tel: Manaton 209. This charity has no set visiting hours. It runs adoption schemes and accepts cigarette vouchers, trading stamps, saddlery and stable equipment in good condition.

The Donkey Sanctuary, Sidmouth, Devon, EX10 0NU. Tel: (01395) 516391 or 578222. Visiting times: every day from 9 am until dusk. Christmas cards by mail order. Fundraising ideas and sponsorship forms, newsletters.

Horses & Ponies Protection Association (HAPPA), (Head Office) 64 Station Road, Padiham, Nr Burnley, Lancashire, BB12 8EF. Tel: (01282) 779138. Visiting times: **Gregory Farm, Brockweir, Nr Chepstow, Gwent, NP6 7NG,** 2 pm–5 pm every day except Monday and Friday. **Capel House, Bullsmoor Lane, Waltham Cross, Hertfordshire, EN1 4RW,** by appointment only. **Shores Hey Farm, Halifax Road, Briercliffe, Nr. Burnley, Lancs, BB10 3QU,** 2 pm–5 pm Saturday and Sunday. The charity has support groups and the HAPPA Club, and schemes for adoption and loan. Gifts and Christmas cards are available by mail order as are fund-raising leaflets, sponsorship forms and advice on organising sponsored rides. HAPPA accepts saddlery, rugs, riding hats and other e   question equipment plus unwanted antiques, paintings andrian good quality collectors' items.

International League for the Protection of Horses (ILPH), (Head Office) Anne Colvin House, Snetterton, Norwich, Norfolk, NR16 2LR. Tel: (01953) 498682. Visiting times: **Hall Farm, Snetterton, Norfolk,** 2.30 pm–4 pm Wednesdays and Sundays. **Overa House Farm, Larling, Norfolk,** 2.30 pm–4 pm Wednesdays and Sundays. **Belwade Farm, Aboyne, Aberdeenshire,** Wednesday afternoons and weekends. **Cherry Tree Farm, Newchapel, Nr Lingfield, Surrey,** 2 pm–4 pm Wednesdays, Thursdays and Sundays. ILPH has an adoption scheme, a Junior Club, and gifts and cards are available by mail order. Help and advice is given on fundraising activities and materials such as posters, leaflets, rosettes and other items.

Lluest Horse & Pony Trust, Beili Bedw Farm, Llanddeusant, Nr Llangadog, Dyfed, SA19 9TG. Visiting times: On specific open days only, but supporters are welcome to visit if they telephone first on (01550) 4661. There is an adoption scheme and Junior Club; children are welcome to spend the day by prior arrangement and with parents' permission. Cards and gifts available by mail order. Fundraising ideas include 'sponsor a brick' (for new stabling) and sponsored ragwort digs.

Redwings Horse Sanctuary, Hill Top Farm, Hall Lane, Frettenham, Norwich, NR12 7LT. Tel: (01603) 737432. Visiting on open days only. The charity runs adoption schemes, a Junior Club (Redwings Rangers), and accepts foreign coins, petrol tokens, bric-a-brac and plants for stalls. Extensive selection of gifts and cards available by mail order.

Tettenhall Horse Sanctuary, Jenny Walker Lane, Old Perton, Wolverhampton, WV6 7HB. Tel: (01902) 764422. Visiting times: 12 noon to 4 pm Sundays or by appointment. The sponsorship scheme is for horses and also for other animals. The charity accepts bric-a-brac, pet foods, blankets, tack, home-made cakes etc. for tombola and sales stalls.

GALLOPING HORSES

Flick books used to be popular toys, but you don't see them for sale nowadays. However, if you have a little patience it is very easy to make your own.

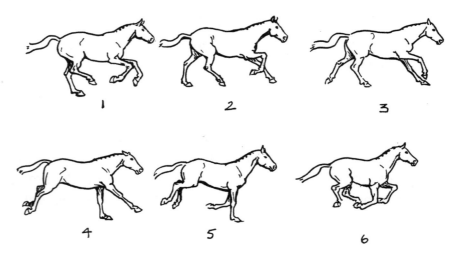

Copy or trace each of the pictures onto a sheet of clean paper. Then cut them out and glue one on each page of a notebook.
Keep the pictures in the right sequence!

Flick through the pages to make the drawings come to life!

The pictures shown here are of a horse galloping. Copy or trace them all onto a clean sheet of paper four times (or more if you have the patience) and then cut them out.

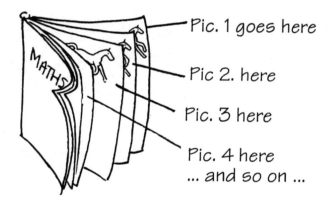

Pic. 1 goes here

Pic 2. here

Pic. 3 here

Pic. 4 here
... and so on ...

Now stick the pictures on the top right-hand page of a notebook (don't use a school exercise book unless you want to get into trouble!), sticking the first picture in the sequence onto the back page, the second picture on the next pag and so forth, working your way towards the front of the book and making sure you keep them in the right order. When you have finished, flick through the book from the back to the front and you will see the horse suddenly come to life and gallop across the top of the pages. You can make up your own flick book showing a horse walking, trotting or even jumping if you like. Use reference books and magazine pictures which show how a horse moves so you get the legs in the right places.

NEAT EATS

If you're really at a loose end, why not try your hand at making some food with a horsy theme, and then inviting some friends round to help you eat it all. Cooking needn't be complicated or difficult so long as you remember to measure out all the ingredients properly and follow the instructions in the right order. Be careful when melting or baking ingredients, use oven gloves when holding hot tins and don't put anything hot directly on top of unprotected surfaces. Before starting, do get permission to use the cooker and ask an adult to help you. Don't leave the kitchen in a mess afterwards, remember to wash up and tidy away everything you have used.

MUCKHEAP CAKES

Once you've made these you'll see just why they're called muckheap cakes, but they're really delicious provided you aren't squeamish.

YOU WILL NEED:
2 Shredded Wheats
2 cups cornflakes
170 gm (6 oz) plain chocolate (broken in small pieces)
2 tablespoons butter
2 tablespoons golden syrup
2 tablespoons sugar
2 tablespoons unsweetened cocoa powder

Put the cornflakes into a mixing bowl and lightly crush them by scrunching them between your fingers; add the Shredded Wheats, breaking them up as you do so. Then put the chocolate, butter, syrup, sugar and cocoa into a saucepan and melt them together, stirring well. Use a very gentle heat – don't be impatient – and remove from the heat as soon as everything has melted or the chocolate will overcook. Pour the mixture over the Shredded Wheat and cornflakes and mix well. Finally, spoon into paper cake cases and leave in the fridge to set.

MUCKHEAP CAKES

Carefully spoon mixture into individual paper cases and allow to cool.

MINTY HORSESHOES

Packed in a pretty box lined with a lacy paper doily, these can make brilliant presents – provided you can stop yourself from eating them all first!

YOU WILL NEED:
1 large egg white
1/4 teaspoon peppermint essence
340 gm (12 oz) sieved icing sugar

Seperate the egg white from the yolk; this involves carefully cracking the shell against the edge of a bowl followed by a bit of careful juggling as you tip the contents from one half of the shell to the other, keeping the yellow yolk in the shells and allowing the white to trickle out into the container. As it can be tricky, you might find it best to ask an adult to help you with this part. Put the egg white and peppermint essence into a bowl, then gradually stir in the icing sugar, a little at a time, until a stiff paste is formed. Knead the mixture until it is smooth. Lightly dust a board and a rolling pin with more sieved icing sugar and carefully roll out to about 6 mm (1/4 in) thick.

Dust a board and the rolling pin with sieved icing sugar before rolling out the peppermint mixture.

Now for the fiddly bit. Using the tip of a knife cut out horseshoe shapes; be patient because it will take you a little while. Then transfer them to a piece of non-stick or waxed paper and leave them to dry overnight. If you feel particularly artistic, try melting some plain chocolate in a bowl over hot water and pouring it into a piping bag fitted with a small plain nozzle; you can then add little blobs to look like nail holes.

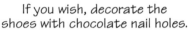

If you wish, decorate the shoes with chocolate nail holes.

Use the tip of a knife to cut out horseshoe shapes.

OAT FINGERS

Oats aren't just for horses, they can make scrumptious biscuits too, but don't raid the feed bin, use rolled oats from the supermarket instead (the sort you use for making porridge).

YOU WILL NEED:
85 gm (3 oz) butter
85 gm (3 oz) soft brown sugar
113 gm (4 oz) rolled oats

Melt the butter in a saucepan over a gentle heat, then add the sugar and stir until it has dissolved. Remove from the heat, pour in the oats and mix thoroughly.

OAT FINGERS

Make sure you always mix all the ingredients together really well

Press the mixture into a lightly greased, shallow 18 cm (7 in) square cake tin and smooth the top. Bake in the centre of an oven, which has been preheated to 220 °C/425 °F/gas mark 7, for 15 minutes until golden brown. Leave to cool slightly, then mark into fingers with a knife and loosen the edges. Once the mixture is firm, turn out onto a wire rack, break into fingers and leave to cool completely.

Use a knife to cut the cooked oat finger mixture into slices

TO MAKE LUXURY OAT FINGERS

Dip the ends of the oat fingers into a bowl of melted chocolate and allow to cool

Do not allow the water to overflow into the bowl of chocolate!

Tip:
To melt chocolate, break into small pieces and place in a heat proof bowl. Place the bowl in a saucepan of water over a low heat until melted.

If you want to make them extra delicious, break 85 gm (3 oz) of plain or milk chocolate into squares and place in a heatproof bowl. Place the bowl in a saucepan of water over a low heat, taking care not to allow the water to overflow into the chocolate. When it has completely melted dip the ends of the cooled oat fingers into the chocolate and allow to cool before eating.

PLANNING AHEAD

Just because you don't have a pony now, it doesn't mean that you're never going to get one, even though you may have to wait a few years before you realise your dreams. In the meantime learn all you can about horses and ponies by reading books and magazines, and try to get as much practical experience beneath your belt as possible by having lessons and perhaps asking if you can become a weekend and holiday helper at your riding school. You could try grovelling to pony owning friends for the occasional ride too, but don't overdo it or else they'll stop being sympathetic about your ponyless state and start hiding behind the muckheap instead when they see you coming. If you do manage to get a ride, avoid being bossy or critical and telling your friend just how the pony should be ridden or cared for. Make the most of the ride (but without wearing the pony to a frazzle or outstaying your welcome) and offer to lend a hand with the stable chores beforehand and afterwards. It's all invaluable experience (and will ensure that you get asked again!).

Plan ahead for when you get a pony of your own - ask for useful birthday and Xmas presents such as buckets, leadropes and haynets

You can plan ahead for the day you do finally take delivery of the equine of your dreams in other practical ways such as beginning to collect together a few bits and pieces ready for him, although you may get a few strange looks when you ask for something like a feed bucket for your birthday! The cost of kitting out a new pony can be horrific, but if you've already been able to buy some of the essentials in advance and over a period of time, it will help to soften the blow to your pocket.

Be sensible about the things you choose; feedstuffs will obviously go off after a while, and saddles, bridles, bits and headcollars may not fit your pony (or horse if you grow a lot whilst waiting). Have a look round a saddlers and you'll find plenty of things you can buy in advance; choose items such as the following.

Grooming kit
Haynets
Leadropes
Bandages
Buckle guards
Plaiting equipment

Sponges for tack cleaning
Bridle hook
Water and feed buckets
Fillet strings
Adjustable one-size fly fringe

Mucking out tools: fork, shovel, broom, skep and wheelbarrow.
Non-perishable first-aid items such as gamgee, thermometer, scissors.

BLINDING BINDINGS

Impress your teachers with the way you take care of school books by covering them with protective jackets to stop them becoming grubby and dog-eared (well, that's the official excuse!). Create a collage of horsy pictures cut from magazines, gluing them onto a large sheet of paper; leftover wallpaper or brown parcel paper is ideal, because it's fairly tough.

1. Glue lots of horsy pictures cut out from magazines onto a large sheet of paper - it doesn't matter if they overlap each other

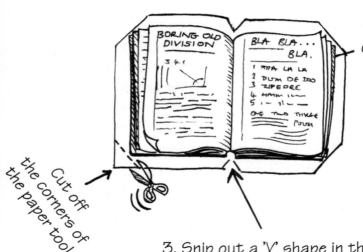

2. Place the book you want to cover on top of the plain side of the paper

Cut off the corners of the paper too!

3. Snip out a 'V' shape in the paper where the spine of the book will be

4. Fold down the overlapping edges of the paper over the book cover

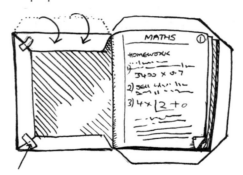

5. Sellotape the corners to secure

When you have completely covered the paper, cut it to the size you want and use it to make a dust jacket. If you're anxious not to spoil your work of art, cover it with a sheet of transparent sticky-backed plastic. Loose ring binders for keeping notes in can be jazzed up and personalised in the same way, by gluing pictures directly onto them.

SHADOW PONIES

Have you noticed the way everyday objects cast spooky shadows on walls? You can make a shadow pony very easily by just using your hands; all you need to do is shape them as shown in the picture, in front of a strong light. Shine the light against a plain wall for the best effect, but don't get your hands too close to the light source because, apart from burning yourself, the outlines will be blurred.

Make a horse-head shadow by holding your hand in front of a light, like this. You will need to dim or turn off overhead room lights first.

Once you have the right shape, you can waggle the ears by moving your thumbs, and make your shadow pony open and close its mouth by moving your little fingers up and down.

There are plenty of horsy places of interest to visit when you're away on holiday or if you're at a loose end at weekends. Although a lot of the places mentioned here are heavy-horse centres, many of them have additional attractions (and other types of horses and ponies), so visiting them can be a fun day out for the whole family. If the places which are mentioned here aren't close enough to visit, don't despair. This isn't an exhaustive list by any means; by checking in the local press, library, or by visiting the local Tourist Information Centre you can find out about other horsy places to visit. Before dropping in, do ring first to check on opening times!

There are lots of horsy places to visit all over the country where you can meet everything from a Shetland to a Shire

The Dorset Heavy Horse Centre, Brambles Farm, Edmondsham, Verwood, Dorset. Tel: (01202) 824040.

The Home of Rest for Horses, Westcroft Stables, Speen Farm, Nr Lacey Green, Aylesbury, Bucks, HP17 0PP. Tel: (01494) 488464.

The National Stud, Newmarket, Suffolk, CB8 0XE. Tel: (01638) 663464.

The Working Carriage Museum, Red House Stables, Old Road, Darley Dale, Matlock, Derbyshire, DE4 2ER. Tel: (01629) 733583.

The Donkey Sanctuary, The International Donkey Protection Trust and The Slade Centre, Slade House, Salcombe Regis, Sidmouth, Devon, EX10 0NU. Tel: (01395) 578222.

Shetland and Small Animal Rescue, Dan's Farm, Ramsbrook Lane, Hale, Merseyside, L24 5RP. Tel: 0151-425 4627.

The National Shire Horse Centre, Yealmpton, Plymouth, PL8 2EL. Tel: (01752) 880268

The Courage Shire Horse Centre, Cherry Garden Lane, Maidenhead Thicket, Maidenhead, Berkshire, SL6 3QD. Tel: (01628) 824848.

The Bass Museum, Horninglow Street, Burton upon Trent, Staffordshire, DE14 1JZ. Tel: (01283) 42031.

The Miniature Pony Centre, Wormhill Farm, North Bovey, Moretonhampstead, Devon, TQ13 8RG. Tel: (01647) 432400.

Valiants Shire World, Lancaster Road, Out Rawcliffe, Nr Blackpool, Lancashire, PR3 6BL. Tel: (01995) 71033.

Northern Shire Horse Centre and Museum, Flower Hill Farm, North Newbald, York, YO4 3TG. Tel: (01430) 827480.

The National Horseracing Museum, 99 High Street, Newmarket, Suffolk, CB8 8JL. Tel: (01638) 667333.

Northcote Heavy Horse Centre, Great Steeping, Nr Spilsby, Lincolnshire, PE23 5PS. Tel: (01754) 86286.

Norfolk Shire Horse Centre, West Runton Riding Stables, Cromer, Norfolk, NR27 9QH. Tel: (01263) 837339.

Olympia Showjumping Championships: held in December, just before Christmas each year – keep an eye out in the national and equestrian press for booking details. There are lots of entertaining novelty events as well as serious jumping classes, so the rest of your family certainly won't be bored.

Stratford Shire Horse Centre, Clifford Road, Stratford upon Avon, Warwickshire, CV37 8HW. Tel: (01789) 266276.

The Royal Mews, Queens Gallery, Buckingham Palace, Buckingham Palace Road, London, SW1A 1AA. Tel: 0171–930 4832.

QUICK DRAW

Learning to draw horses and ponies is not as difficult as you might think, although it might take a little patience and practice for you to perfect it. Start off with a pencil, to ensure that if you go wrong you can rub out and correct your mistakes easily. With experience you can experiment with the use of other mediums and techniques to produce all sorts of effects.

SIDE VIEW   FRONT VIEW

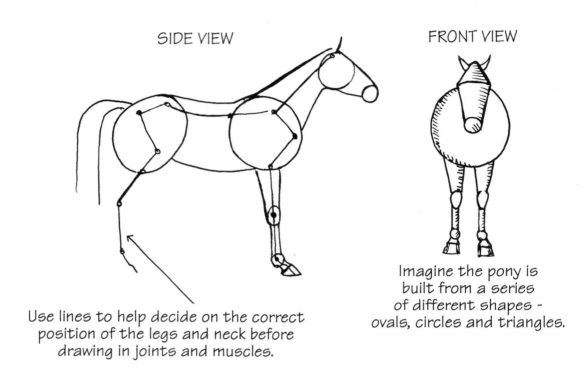

Use lines to help decide on the correct position of the legs and neck before drawing in joints and muscles.

Imagine the pony is built from a series of different shapes - ovals, circles and triangles.

Don't press too hard with the pencil because it will be difficult to erase mistakes, and don't be too quick to use your rubber; try to get a general outline or impression down before you start to fill in any details. As a pony-mad person you should have a head start since you will have some idea of a pony's shape, where all the joints are and in which direction they bend, but you will still need to study your subject carefully. All ponies have slightly different shapes and proportions; some may be chunky in build with short legs, whilst others may be more delicately built, and your drawing should reflect such individual characteristics if you are doing a picture of a particular pony. Even if you are drawing an imaginary pony, remember that a cheeky, hairy pony head will look strange if combined with long, slim racehorse legs.

If you don't have a real horse or pony to study, look at photos, but don't cheat and trace them or you'll never really learn to draw them properly. You may find it easier to get the basic shape right by dividing the body up into a series of different shapes, such as ovals, circles and triangles.

As a rough guideline,
the body of the average pony
should fit into a square

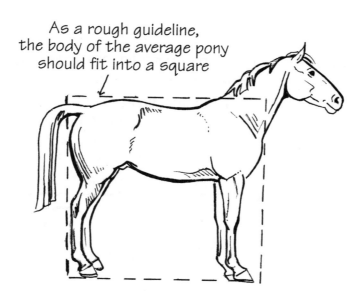

Drawing horses and ponies in motion is more difficult than drawing them standing still, and this is where looking at photos is especially helpful because it can be very difficult to see exactly what the sequence of movement of legs is, particularly when the pony is moving at speed. Don't forget that the head carriage may also change.

Lower the headcarriage
for a galloping pony

- and raise it to show
collection or excitement.

Practise drawing movement
using simple lines to capture
the pony's outline
at different
paces.

Use photos as a guide
- but don't trace them.

PONY PUPPETS

Nothing could be easier to make than pony finger puppets. Make a paper pattern first by drawing around the outline of your index finger, leaving a 1.3 cm (1/2 in) margin all round it. Then add on a stylized head to the fingertip end, and cut it out. Place the pattern on a square of felt and draw round it with a felt tip pen, then cut it out and make another just the same.

1. Make a paper pattern by drawing round your finger, then adding a stylized head

leave a 1.3 cm (1/2") margin

2. Use the paper pattern to cut out two felt shapes, then stitch around the edges. When you have finished, turn it inside out to hide the seam.

leave a hole at the bottom for your finger

Stitch along the edges of the head and neck (but leave the bottom open because this is where you'll put your finger!) and then carefully turn it inside out. Cut out two triangles of felt for the ears and two small circles of a contrasting colour of felt for the eyes, then glue them in place. Finally, push a little cotton wool into the end of the nose. As a finishing touch, glue a short strip of fun-fur fabric along the neck for the mane.Because they are so quick,easy and cheap to make, you can create a whole stableful of characters, and maybe some for your friends too.

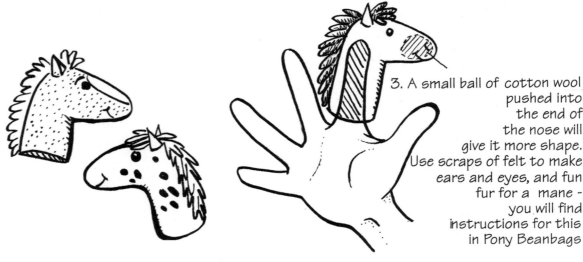

3. A small ball of cotton wool pushed into the end of the nose will give it more shape. Use scraps of felt to make ears and eyes, and fun fur for a mane - you will find instructions for this in Pony Beanbags

BUZZ OFF

Ponies with sparse forelocks will welcome a fly fringe in the summer to help keep winged pests out of their eyes. They are very easy to make. All you need is an old browband (you can quite often buy second-hand ones cheaply at saddlers; it doesn't need to be smart, just serviceable). Alternatively you could make your own from a strip of material doubled over with the edges stitched up, but don't forget that you will need to make it long enough to turn the ends over to form loops through which you slot the headpiece of the headcollar. Next, gather together some lengths of string and simply loop them along the browband as shown. What could be simpler?

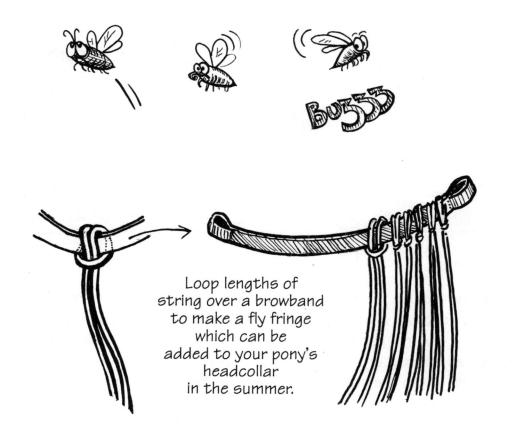

Loop lengths of string over a browband to make a fly fringe which can be added to your pony's headcollar in the summer.

IMPROVE YOUR RIDING (WITHOUT A PONY!)

Sometimes it's hard to believe that your riding will ever improve when the only chance you get to sit on a pony is that precious lesson once a week. What's more, it seems that no sooner have you scrambled on board than the time has passed in a flash, and that's it until next time!

Even if you are lucky enough to own a pony, you may not always get a chance to ride as often as you would like, especially during the winter when it's too dark to ride before or after school, and you're restricted to weekends.

Still, it's no good sitting around moaning about it, there are loads of things you can do to help improve your riding in the meantime, and you don't even need a pony to do them. Take reading for a start. I know there is no substitute for the real thing, but it does help if you have some kind of grasp of what you are trying to achieve when in the saddle and why. There are loads of really good books around which will explain all the theory involved and how to get better results from the ponies you ride. What else? Well, you could try the following.

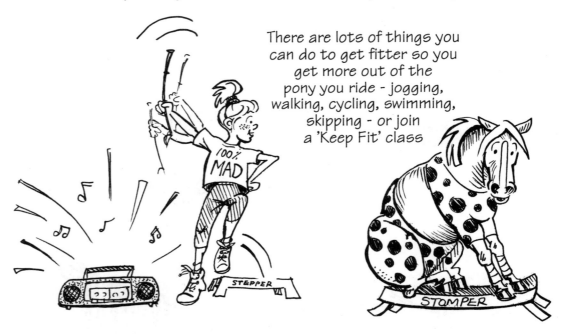

There are lots of things you can do to get fitter so you get more out of the pony you ride - jogging, walking, cycling, swimming, skipping - or join a 'Keep Fit' class

GET FIT

There's no excuse for not being fit enough to get the best from the pony you ride; you certainly will not get the best from him if you're puffing and panting after just a few minutes in trot. Jogging, brisk walking, swimming, cycling, skipping will all boost your level of fitness, so get going. Do take care with exercise if you suffer from a medical problem or disorder; get fit by all means, but ask your doctor for advice first.

ALL CHANGE

Practise changing your whip over properly, and getting used to carrying it in both hands without it feeling awkward. Tie a long piece of string to the arms of a chair to act as reins and sit or stand behind it. Hold the 'reins' and your whip as you would normally and practise putting them into one hand and changing your whip over correctly whilst keeping a level contact. You can also practise lengthening and shortening your reins without fumbling or dropping them.

Tie a long piece of string to the back of a chair for 'reins' and practise holding them in both hands, one hand, and changing your whip over without dropping it.

LOOK AND LEARN

Although it is nicer to be riding yourself, you can still learn a lot by watching other people have their lessons. There are loads of tips to be picked up by seeing the sort of mistakes other riders make (you'll probably be able to identify some of your own) and listening to the instructor's advice for correcting them. Lots of riding schools have floodlit riding areas, so it is possible to watch lessons even when it is dark outside.

TAKE NOTE

Buy a small notebook and, after your lessons, jot down any comments your instructor has made which you found especially helpful or effective so you don't forget them. Read through what you have written before your next lesson so you know what you will have to work on most.

LOOSEN UP

Doing a few exercises at home in between lessons, or before you ride, can do a lot to help you loosen up and become more supple which, in turn, should help your position to improve (and you might even find that you don't ache so much afterwards!). Even couch potatoes will find that it's not such hard work as it sounds because there are exercises you can do sitting in a chair watching the television! There are other exercises you can do, as well the ones mentioned below which can be geared towards helping overcome any specific problems you have when riding – ask your instructor about them.

Each exercise can be done three or four times but don't try to do too much, or you will undo all the good you have done.

Don't forget that if you have a medical problem or disability you should check with your doctor first before doing any exercises.

HEAD ROLL. Let your head tilt forward, then slowly roll it from side to side.

Tip: Don't grit your teeth - keep your jaw relaxed.

HEAD ROLL

Ease tension in your neck by allowing your head to tilt forwards so your chin rests on your chest; gently and slowly roll your head from side to side, trying to keep your jaw relaxed (imagine you are chewing gum if necessary). Do not roll your head in a backwards direction because, apart from the fact that it won't be particularly beneficial, it could be injurious.

SHOULDER SHRUG. Hunch up both shoulders, then roll them backwards and downwards.

(This exercise is good for round shouldered riders)

SHOULDER SHRUG

This is a good one for people who tend to be round shouldered and hunch up when riding. Lift both shoulders up beneath your ears, then roll them backwards and downwards, breathing out as you do so.

ELBOW PUSH

Another good exercise for slouchers. Hold both arms in front of you at shoulder height, with the elbows bent and finger tips touching. Push both elbows back as far as they will go, keeping your arms parallel to the ground. You should be able to feel how it makes you stretch through the front of your ribcage.

ELBOW PUSH. Hold both arms in front of you, finger tips touching - then slowly push both elbows backwards

ARM CIRCLES

Slowly circle each arm alternately, swinging it in a backwards direction to help loosen your shoulders. As each arm moves up above your head, stretch up through your ribcage.

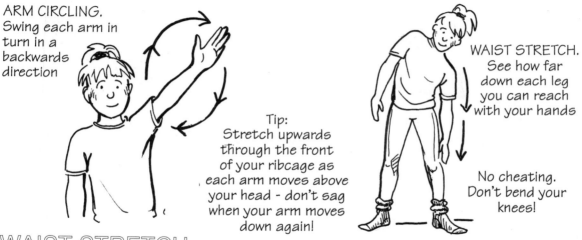

ARM CIRCLING. Swing each arm in turn in a backwards direction

Tip: Stretch upwards through the front of your ribcage as each arm moves above your head - don't sag when your arm moves down again!

WAIST STRETCH. See how far down each leg you can reach with your hands

No cheating. Don't bend your knees!

WAIST STRETCH

Stand upright, feet spaced apart and your hands hanging down by your sides. Slide your left hand as far down your left leg as you can reach, by inching your body over in that direction – no cheating by bending your knees.

This exercise is good for stiff ankles

ANKLE CIRCLING. Circle both ankles in clockwise and anti-clockwise directions

ANKLE CIRCLING

This is good for those of you with stiff ankles. While sitting down, rotate your ankles in both clockwise and anticlockwise directions.

THIGH STRETCH

If you have trouble mounting, stand in front of a chair with one foot on the seat (take your muddy wellies off first!), lean forwards over the knee of the raised foot, keeping the other heel flat on the ground and then straighten up again. This also helps to stretch the calf muscle of the supporting leg. It is not as easy as it sounds so don't overdo it to start with but just stretch forward as far as is comfortable.

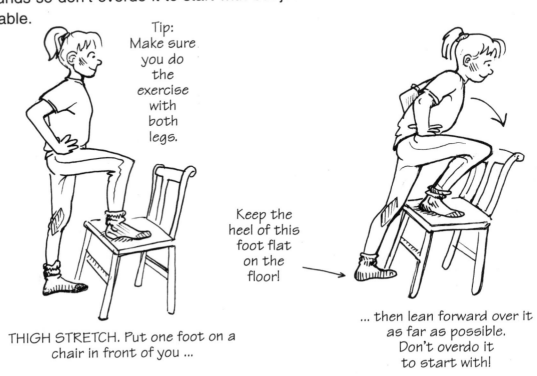

Tip: Make sure you do the exercise with both legs.

Keep the heel of this foot flat on the floor!

THIGH STRETCH. Put one foot on a chair in front of you ...

... then lean forward over it as far as possible. Don't overdo it to start with!

JOIN THE CLUB

If you wanted to join a club of some kind, but weren't quite sure who to contact, or what was involved, look no further! Joining a club is a great way of making new friends, improving your riding, learning more about caring for ponies, and having fun at the same time. There are several organisations you could contact for further details, but do remember to enclose a large stamped addressed envelope when writing.

THE PONY CLUB

The Pony Club is a world-wide organisation with 366 branches in the UK and 1812 branches in countries overseas; anyone under the age of 21 years can join, although those who are 18 and over are known as Associate members. All sorts of activities are organised, including competitions of all kinds, polo, lectures, mounted rallies, visits to places of interest and shows, tests, summer camps, not to mention fund raising and social events such as barbeques and discos. You don't have to own a pony in order to join, but you will get the most benefit from the Pony Club if you can hire or borrow a pony for mounted rallies from a local riding school.

Further details: The Pony Club, British Equestrian Centre, Stoneleigh, Kenilworth, Warwickshire, CV8 2LR.

THE HORSE RANGERS ASSOCIATION

The Horse Ranger movement was founded by Raymond Gordon in 1954 to enable young people to learn how to ride, look after their horses and ponies, and generally to be nicer, caring people. There are two sections: eight to ten-year-old members are called Ponies, whilst those of 11 and over are the Horse Rangers. There is a distinct military feel to the Association, with the use of 'officers' and a smart, stylish uniform of beige jodhs, black boots, coloured shirt, scarf and lanyard; BSI standard hats are worn when riding, with a Canadian-style felt hat to complete the dress uniform. There are troops currently located at Epping, Dorking, Windsor, Sevenoaks, Harwich, and the Isle of Bute in Scotland, with the headquarters and training centre based at Hampton Court Palace. Two of the troops have their own horses and ponies but others are attached to riding establishments. Membership is restricted to those without ponies and there is always a waiting list of people who want to join, so if you are interested, write for further details now.

The Horse Rangers Association, c/o The Royal Mews, Hampton Court Palace, East Molesey, Surrey, KT8 9BW.

RIDING SCHOOL CLUBS

If your riding school doesn't run an internal club, perhaps they would consider it if you made the suggestion. One evening set aside for club members, with instruction plus a lecture or video either before or after the lesson would doubtless be popular (as well as being profitable for the school). In addition, the club members could get together to go on visits to equine places of interest and to major shows; discount on show tickets can often be gained by buying blocks of tickets rather than individual tickets.

MAGAZINE CLUBS

There are two major childrens's/teenage horsy magazines in the UK that you can subscribe to even if you live overseas and both run special clubs for their readers. You don't have to own a pony in order to join – or even be able to ride regularly – you just have to be mad about horses and ponies.

On joining the *Pony* magazine club you are sent lots of items inside a special club wallet including a membership passport with your personal club number, a button badge, rosette, Thelwell ruler and rubber, an autographed print of a top rider and a sticker set. There are special members-only competitions and free gifts, and a birthday draw each month when five members receive a special present. By collecting coupons you can also send off for free rosettes to add to your collection. If you fancy the idea of a horsy penfriend to write to, you will find a list of people who can be contacted via the magazine on the readers' letters page. Details of the club and membership forms can be found on the club pages of *Pony* magazine, which is published monthly.

Horse & Pony magazine, which is published fortnightly, runs the Young Riders' Club for readers under the age of 18; membership will bring you a welcoming letter, a Freddie Fact File and photo (Freddie is *Horse & Pony's* own pony), stickers, a membership card, wallet, badge, key ring, pen, reflexite dots and a rosette. Only contributions from YRC members are published on the club pages and there are special members-only competitions to enter each month. You can also find a horsy penpal through the magazine by ringing a special number which you will find printed in the magazine, as well as details and a membership form for joining the club.

Both the magazines are available from most newsagents but if you have trouble tracking-down copies (or getting hold of them regularly) you could always ask for a yearly subscription as a Christmas or birthday present. The addresses to write to are:

Pony magazine
Haslemere House,
Lower Street,
Haslemere,
GU27 2PE

Horse & Pony magazine,
Bretton Court,
Bretton,
Peterborough,
PE3 8DZ.

Make new friends - try joining
a horsy club

If you thought stamp collecting was boring, perhaps it's because you didn't realise just how many horsy stamps there are to collect – literally thousands. Collecting just one type of stamp – those featuring horses for example – is called 'thematic' collecting because your collection has a particular theme.

First things first. While you don't need a huge amount of expensive equipment, some items are essential for handling and inspecting your collection without damaging it. You can either buy a stamp collector's starter kit with all the necessary bits and pieces from a stamp shop (or a good stationers) or, alternatively, buy them separately. The essentials are a stamp album, stamp hinges, a magnifying glass, and tweezers. Tweezers are vital because stamps should not be handled more than necessary, however clean your hands may look. They should be flat-ended tweezers, not the ridged ones used for pulling splinters out of your fingers.

A magnifying glass will allow you to look at your collection more closely; stamps aren't very big, and you won't be able to see the more minute details without one. Stamp hinges affix the stamps to the pages of your stamp album without damaging them, and ensure they can be easily viewed.

There are several ways of collecting stamps: you will find them for sale at stamp shops, at jumble sales, you can buy them by mail order from dealers, or arrange swaps with friends. And don't forget to keep an eye out for new issues of stamps at the Post Office. Sometimes you will also find special stamp fairs advertised in local newspapers. Stamp dealers selling by mail order advertise in magazines, and if you look in your local *Yellow Pages* under 'Stamp Dealers' you might find there is a stamp shop near you.

Another good way of collecting stamps (and of finding out more about them) is to join a local stamp collector's club – there may be one at your school, or you could ask at your local library. Most clubs will have a junior section. If you want to find out more about stamps on your favourite subject, most libraries will have a selection of books and catalogues you can look through.

CARPET-KEPT PONIES

The great thing about collecting model horses and ponies is that you can have any breed you like, and as many as you want (within reason). There are no problems with bills for feed or field rent, and what's more you don't have to get up early every morning to muck out, or worry about going away on holiday. You can actually learn quite a lot about things like conformation, breed lines, stable management and equipment by building up a model collection with all the accessories.

If you can't have a real pony, models can be the next best thing, especially if you join a model club because then you will be able to make new friends and enter competitions as well as exchanging news and views and making swaps.

You can even take part in model shows, so not owning a pony needn't be a bar to winning a few rosettes if you are the competitive type. At 'live' shows owners gather with their models and enter classes ranging from in-hand showing to ridden equitation, just like a proper show but on a smaller scale. There are two other types of model horse show: postal and photo shows. With postal shows you send details of the model – its name, height, breed and so on – to the organiser. After that it's a matter of luck because the winners are picked out of a hat. Photo shows require more skill. You send a photo of the model to the organiser, and the entries are judged on points like how good the conformation is, whether the colours are right for the breed, neatness and turnout.

You can either buy models and accessories, or make your own using self-hardening or bake-in-the-oven modelling clay but the easiest way to start a collection is to buy the models.

Build up a collection of model horses and ponies - you could join a club and even enter shows with them.

Julip models are the ones with the bendy legs and long flowing manes and tails which you can groom and trim to the length you want. The riders also have bendy legs which help keep them in position. There are several different models and riders with accessories. The company also runs the Julip Pony Club; members receive a membership card, club rosette, notelets, and a quarterly magazine with free offers, articles on pony care, a special members' page, and the chance to win Julip models in regular competitions. For a brochure and price list write to: Julip Ltd., Evershot, Dorchester, Dorset, DT2 0JY. Tel: (01935) 83348.

Magpie Models have an extensive range of $\frac{1}{12}$th scale model ponies, hunters and Arabs (and foals) in a wide range of colours, plus the 'Dream Pony' collectors' models, all with silky manes and tails to groom and plait. A large selection of headcollars, rugs, numnahs, black leather saddles and bridles, boots, stables, show jumps and other accessories are also available. For a brochure and price list, contact: Magpie Models, Middle Humber Stables, Bishopsteignton, South Devon, TQ14 9TD. Tel: (01626) 773240.

Breyer have been making model horses for 40 years and now have such a huge variety to choose from – ranging from Arabs and Appaloosas to Lipizzaners and Hanoverians – that you won't know which to choose first. Made from tenite, a special very strong plastic, they are all individually hand-painted. Riders and a small line of accessories are also available. Brochure and price list from: Breyer Model Horses, The Wentworth Collection, 10 Tennyson Road, Brentwood, Essex, CM13 2SP.

Country Style Models do not have a club, but there are plenty of special offers on various items plus gift packs at Christmas. There are three horse and pony models to choose from, a rider and some very realistic accessories including buildings, bandages, show jumps, rugs, mucking out equipment, haynets, bedding (and even some incredibly lifelike imitation piles of droppings). You can obtain more information from: C.S.M, PO Box 35, Carmarthen, Dyfed. Tel: (01267) 202273.

If you fancy having a go at making your own model horses or ponies, Apis Model Kits supply everything you need (bar scissors and kapok stuffing) in kit form to make some lovely scale characters in felt. All the models have bead eyes, and a wire frame so that once finished they can gently be posed in realistic positions. Although you may find you need some help from an adult, no special sewing skills are needed, full assembly instructions are provided, and the end results are well worth the effort. Further details can be obtained by sending a stamped addressed envelope to: Apis Model Kits, 3 Dovedale Road, Wallasey, Merseyside, L45 0LP.

Model Horses Unlimited is a club. Members get free monthly newsletters containing club and model news and lots of shows. Other benefits include: a list of members, model horse studs, free unclassified advertising, a grading scheme for models with certificates, ribbons and rosettes. A magazine full of extra information is published three times a year and is available to members only. If you would like more details, send a stamped, self-addressed envelope to: Model Horses Unlimited, 5 Brington Road, Long Buckby, Northamptonshire, NN6 7RW. When writing the first time, please mark the top left corner of your envelope 'HB'.

NAMEPLATE

A smart nameplate on your pony's stable door will make him look really important (which he is). If you don't have a pony of your own, there is no reason why you shouldn't make one for your favourite pony at the riding school (with the owner's permission), or for a friend's pony. Its fairly easy to make although you may also need some help from an adult.

1. Ask an adult to cut a piece of wood to the right length and width. Sandpaper off any rough edges.

2. Paint or stencil your pony's name on the wood. Use a clear varnish when the paint is dry to weatherproof it.

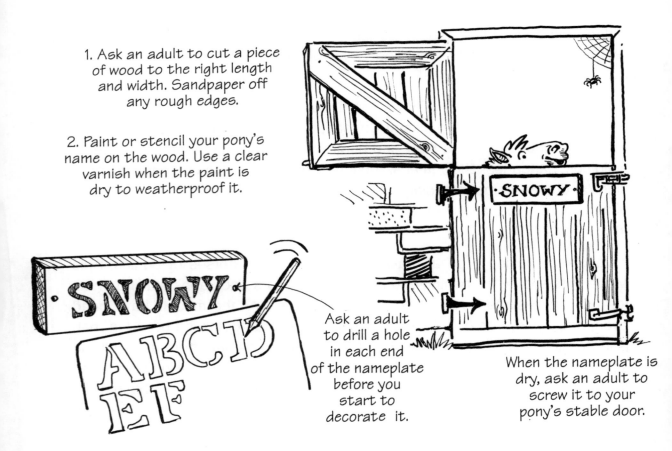

Ask an adult to drill a hole in each end of the nameplate before you start to decorate it.

When the nameplate is dry, ask an adult to screw it to your pony's stable door.

To start with you'll need a piece of wood approximately 30.5 cm × 9 cm (12 in × $3\frac{1}{2}$ in) in size (bigger if it's a very long name) and between 1.3 cm–2 cm ($\frac{1}{2}$ in– $\frac{3}{4}$ in) thick. It doesn't need to be a really good piece; an offcut will do. Ask your dad if he has anything suitable, and to cut it to the right size for you. If you don't have anything at home, you can buy a piece cut to the right size from DIY stores.

The next job is to ask an adult to drill a hole in each end so that once you have finished your nameplate it can be screwed securely to (or over) the stable door. You can then sandpaper any rough edges.

Either leave the surface natural, or give it a coat of emulsion paint and leave it to dry before starting the lettering. It is a good idea to roughly mark out the letters in pencil first, so that you make sure they all fit in (and that the spelling is correct). If you find that your lettering isn't very neat, use stencils instead. Carefully paint inside the pencilled outlines using a fine paintbrush and either emulsion, gloss, or even poster paints. Let the paint dry and finally add a coat of clear varnish; let that dry and it is ready to put up.

TAG IT

... punch a hole and thread a piece of ribbon through - then attach to gift!

Carefully cut out horsy pictures from greetings cards ...

Some birthday and Christmas cards you are given have pictures which are just too nice to throw away but, on the other hand, you can't hoard them forever! Put them to practical use by recycling them to make gift tags to attach to presents. Cut out the pictures and make a hole in the card with a paper punch through which you thread a piece of coloured wool or gift tape so it is easy to attach the tag to the present.

PONY PAPERWEIGHTS

Paperweights stop loose notes and bits of paper straying from wherever you put them down. You will need a large, smooth-surfaced stone – preferably one which is flattish on the top and bottom sides. If you can't find a suitable one in the garden, try looking for one the next time you go to the beach. Give it a good scrub so that the surface is clean and leave it to dry. If the stone is a nice colour, you can leave it plain; alternatively, give it a coat of emulsion, but remember to let it dry properly before going onto the next stage!

Paint a picture - or glue on one cut from a magazine - to a clean, heavy, smooth-surfaced stone.

"MINTY" - BORN 10.5.94.

Personalize it by painting a pony's name around the sides.

Find a horsy picture in a magazine and carefully cut around the outline with scissors or a craft knife. Try to choose a picture with well-defined and not over-complicated outlines because this will be easier to cut out accurately.

Glue the picture on to the top surface of the stone, making sure that the glue covers all of the picture, right up to the edges. If you like, you can, using poster paints and a fine brush, paint in names or dates beneath the picture to give a personal touch for special occasions if you are planning to give it as a present. If you have the talent you might prefer to paint a picture on to the stone, rather than using one from a magazine.

When the glue or paint is dry, apply a coat of clear varnish to give it a glossy, professional finish, as well as to protect it.

If you are worried about the paperweight scratching polished surfaces, glue a piece of felt to the underside.

Use your finished paperweight as a doorstop or to prevent loose papers blowing away.

ARMCHAIR RIDER

You don't have to get on a pony in order to learn more about riding, you can, in fact, do it from the comfort of an armchair. This obviously has a certain extra appeal on those nasty, cold, wet winter days. There is a huge range of horsy videos available nowadays covering virtually everything you can think of, from the poised elegance of dressage to the thrills, spills and excitement of cross-country riding – not to mention tapes on all aspects of stable management and pony care. You will find mail order advertisements for them in horsy magazines.

Lots of saddlers sell videos too, but if you find buying them a bit expensive or think that you might only want to watch them a couple of times, enquire whether the saddlers offer a horsy video hire service. If you club together with a couple of friends, it can offer a cheap afternoon's or evening's entertainment. Not having a video recorder could pose a bit of a problem, but if you ask nicely, you are sure to find a friend who won't mind you using theirs.

If you would rather be entertained than educated, but still want to watch something horsy, trot along to your local video hire shop, and browse through the children's or Family Entertainment sections. You can choose from titles such as *International Velvet* (the story of a girl who eventually gains a place on the Olympic three-day-event team) to stories based on real life such as that of steeplechase jockey Bob Champion who, weak and ill from cancer, carries on fighting for his dream of winning the Grand National (*Champions*).

CLIP
CLOP

Even couch potatoes can learn more about ponies and riding without having to stir from the settee!

PERSONALIZED PRESENTS

If you can't think of a useful present to give a pony owning friend, they may appreciate a new body, water or dandy brush for their grooming kit. Buy the sort that has an unvarnished* wooden back and give it a special personalized touch by painting the pony's name (use stencils if you want to make it really neat) plus a picture of the pony on to the brush back. Apply a coat of clear varnish over the top, being careful not to let it run into the bristles. If you have the patience, you could also personalize all your own grooming kit like this, then you will always be able to track it down if someone else 'borrows' it !

Use your imagination to create a personalized present for a friend by painting names and pictures onto body and dandy brushes.

* **Tip:** If you can't get hold of an unvarnished brush, use a piece of sandpaper to remove the varnish before you try painting on it so that the paint sticks properly.

SPECTATOR SPORTS

You don't have to compete in order to go to shows and have fun. Whatever the venue, be it just the gymkhana down the road, or a major international meeting like Olympia or the Horse of the Year Show, there's lots to learn from watching others. It is as well to be thoroughly prepared before setting off though, if you are going to make the most of a day out.

WHAT TO WEAR

Do wear the right gear for the occasion, and the weather. If you are going to be doing a lot of walking (at a cross-country event for example) then comfortable footwear is going to be vital unless you want to end up nursing gigantic blisters and feeling miserable. If you are at a local show and suspect you might get roped into holding ponies for friends, sensible shoes are a must; open-toed sandals or flip flops might be cool on a hot day but won't do much to protect your feet from metal-shod hooves if you get trodden on.

If the weather is cold, wrap up well and, if it looks a bit uncertain, be on the safe side and take a waterproof outer garment of some kind. Plastic cagoules can be brilliant because, if you don't need it after all, it can be rolled into a small bundle which is easy to carry around.

THINGS TO TAKE

Although you can usually buy refreshments at most shows, it is worth taking some food along; it is cheaper and at least you won't end up being stuck in a mile-long queue when you are starving hungry. A plastic bottle filled with squash is a good idea too. If it is hot, take some sunblock because it is very easy to get burnt without realising it. Don't forget some money in case you have to pay an admission fee to the showground (and you might want an ice cream!).

FINDING OUT ABOUT WHAT IS GOING ON

It helps if you have a basic understanding of the classes you are watching, so, if possible, try to find out about the rules beforehand; there are lots of good books which will explain them.

When you arrive at the showground, pick up a schedule (at smaller local shows they are available from the Secretary's tent, and at big shows there is usually a desk near the entrance where you can get a programme of events) so that you know which classes will be going on where and roughly when they will be starting. Make a note of anything you especially want to see to make sure you don't miss it! Check out the showground, so that you know where all the rings (and the loos) are. There may also be trade stands you might like to browse around, but don't get carried away. Although you can sometimes pick up real bargains, and some of the bigger shows can be good places to find unusual gifts, it can be difficult if you buy something and decide later you want to change it if the retailer has travelled from several counties away!

WHAT TO DO

Having decided which classes you particularly want to watch, make sure you get to the right ring in planty of time to get a good view.

If you are at a cross-country event, don't stay by the same fence the whole time. If you arrive early enough, walk the whole course to see the fences at close quarters and try to decide just how you would tackle them. This will help you to decide which jumps will be the most interesting to watch and where you will want to spend the most time. If it is hilly, you can also discover the best vantage points from where you will be able to see several fences. During the course of the competition move from one fence to the next once you have seen several riders tackling it, but do be careful not to get in the way of competitors or you will spoil everyone's day. Normally you will hear a whistle being blown to warn spectators of a rider's approach, but this isn't always the case at small unaffiliated events, so stay alert.

When watching showing classes study conformation, correct movement, turnout and the art of showing a horse or pony at its best. Try putting yourself in the position of the judge and decide in which order you would place the entries and why; you will need to look closely and concentrate.

If it is permitted, spend some time looking behind the scenes (this isn't always possible at major shows for security reasons) because you can learn a lot from watching exhibits being prepared and warmed up for their classes. Many people at local level are very helpful if you genuinely want to learn more and ask sensible questions, but choose your moment. If someone is obviously in the middle of getting ready for a class, they won't welcome interruptions!

Finally, a word of warning. As a spectator, it is very easy to criticise other people's performances. Whilst in some instances you might be quite correct in your judgement, it is not always wise to express it too loudly; the rider's friend or relative could be standing right next to you!

Spectating at shows can be fun - but make sure you
do not hinder the competitors or get in their way!